REVERSALS

REVERSALS

EVELYN F SUAREZ

ISBN: 979-8-218-47578-9

"I have seen servants upon horses, and princes walking as servants upon the earth."
(Ecclesiastes 10:7 KJV)

Preface

Back in January 2024 I felt a nudge from God that He wanted me to write a retelling of the Book of Esther. To be honest, it was a back-and-forth. I couldn't shake it off. And believe me, I tried. But here I am, having done just that. I am grateful for this opportunity to have answered the call to authorship.

This narrative of the Book of Esther is based on my perspective of the events stated in the scriptures. I know many traditional books include additional details of the story of Esther, but I chose the Bible in the English Standard Version. I enjoy this version because it is simple and easy to understand. After many years of hearing teachings and reading about the story of Esther, I decided to pour into it while in prayer. As a result, here is what I term *"**Reversals**."*

You will notice that there are two narratives. One will follow the story with a brief commentary, and the second will include more in-depth discussion and perceptions. I've included brief character sketches of the five prominent individuals. I trust your life will be enriched and blessed as much as mine.

Table of Contents

ONE

"Now in the days of Ahasuerus, the Ahasuerus who reigned from India to Ethiopia over 127 provinces," (Esther 1:1 ESV).

During his third-year reign, Ahasuerus, king of Persia, held a great feast for his officials and servants. His rulership extended to 127 provinces, from India to Ethiopia. Within this group of officials were his army, the nobles, and all the governors of the provinces. This display of his vast riches lasted for 180 days and presented a means to secure and fortify the unity of his empire. Considering the modes of transportation that existed, it is safe to assume that the slow-moving flow of each arriving headship required such an expanse of time. From the finest linens to precious stones, marble, and couches of gold and silver, the king's court was a magnificent remarkable sight. Royal servants served the wine in gold vessels and other types of goblets. Under the king's orders, there were to be no limits on how much everyone was permitted to drink. Another feast was held for seven days for the rest of his citizens immediately following. King Ahasuerus seemed both extravagant and generous. In addition, Queen Vashti had a feast for the women.

On the seventh day, in an apparent state of intoxication, the king summoned seven of his eunuchs to bring Queen Vashti to show her beauty to those present. But the queen refused to appear, and the king became enraged. He sought counsel to decide what course of action to take with the queen. His counselors suggested that Queen Vashti be deposed and give the royal estate to another. She had disobeyed the king and would cause all women in the kingdom to show disrespect to their husbands. The King was satisfied with the recommendation and ordered it so. Immediately, couriers delivered letters to all the provinces, informing them of the king's decision.

Although this chapter ends on a sour note of permanent separation between the king and queen, we mustn't doubt the adage, "God works in a mysterious way, His wonders to perform." God will use situations to reveal what's in people's hearts. Let me say that Vashti was not in line with God's purposes, and she had to go. God had somebody better suited to combat the future threat to his chosen people.

***

"After these things, when the anger of King Ahasuerus had abated, he remembered Vashti and what she had done and what had been decreed against her" (Esth 2:1).

Over time, King Ahasuerus began to long for Vashti. Maybe he seemed disinterested and lost in his thoughts. Perhaps he couldn't focus. Rightfully discerning what was happening, his attendants came forward with a plan suggesting that all the beautiful young virgins be gathered at the palace. They would undergo a beauty process for 12 months under the guidance of the king's eunuch, Hegai. Then, be presented to him. Whichever of the women pleased his majesty would be crowned queen. The King agreed with the plan, and his servants began preparing. His desire to find a suitable queen demonstrated that he had loved and valued Vashti. His anger was due in part to his broken heart. He hoped things would come together for him. *"Whoso findeth a wife findeth a good thing, and obtaineth favor of the LORD"* (Prov 18:22).

Mordecai, a Jew, is introduced at this moment in the story. He was one of many who had been led into exile along with Jeconiah, king of Judah, by King Nebuchadnezzar of Babylon. Many other Jews had returned to their land, but Mordecai remained in Susa. He raised his cousin Hadassah, an orphan, as his daughter. The name Hadassah means myrtle tree. She was also known as Esther and joined all the young virgins who gathered at the king's palace. It didn't take long for Hegai to favor her highly. Besides physical beauty, her kind and gentle spirit made her stand out, and he provided her with the best diet, cosmetics, and treatments. He also assigned seven handmaidens to her and gave them the best quarters in the king's palace. During this time, she did not reveal to anyone her ancestry, for Mordecai had advised her not to. Every day,

Mordecai would go by the court of the young women to inquire about Esther's state.

The young virgins entered a year of beauty treatments, ranging from special ointments, lotions, oils, and essences to special diets. Although the biblical narrative does not give specific details, I suggest they were instructed in royal protocol, etiquette, manners, and social skill development. It does explicitly mention that each young woman was allowed to take anything she desired to the king's palace. Again, we can assume it could be a particular piece of jewelry or accessory to enhance her beauty in the king's eyes. Each, in turn, would spend an evening with the king and return to the harem under the guardianship of Shaashgaz, another of the king's eunuchs. There, she remained with the rest of the concubines unless the king asked for her again by name.

Four years later, in the seventh year of King Ahasuerus's reign, it was Esther's turn to go before the king. During those four years, anyone who encountered Esther got to know who she was. Her kindness and pure heart touched those around her. Her humility was apparent when she asked Hegai to choose what he thought would suit her. Whether it was a particular garment or adornment remains unknown. But no matter what, she still won the favor of all who saw her. Her encapsulated beauty was a vision of loveliness.

At last, the time had arrived for Esther to be revealed to the king. She was taken to his palace, and the Bible says that the king loved Esther more than all the other women. She found favor and grace in his eyes. He set the royal crown upon her head, and she became queen instead of Vashti. His broken heart healed with the entrance of Esther into his life. A banquet was prepared for all his officials and servants, known as Esther's feast. In addition to the feast, he granted a remission of taxes to the provinces and gave generous gifts. Even after her coronation, Queen Esther did not share her ancestry with anyone because Mordecai advised her not to.

It was after this time that one day, Mordecai was sitting at the king's gate. Two of the king's eunuchs, Bigthan and Teresh, who guarded the threshold, became angry with the king, and planned to assassinate him. Mordecai became aware of the scheme and related it to Queen Esther.

She then told the king in Mordecai's name. Upon investigating the matter and verifying it to be so, the men were both hanged on the gallows. This act was recorded in the book of the Chronicles in the presence of the king.

TWO

"After these things, King Ahasuerus promoted Haman the Agagite, the son of Hammedatha, and advanced him and set his throne above all the officials who were with him" (Esth 3:1).

Four years passed, and the king promoted Haman the Agagite to Prime Minister. Because of his position, everyone was obliged to bow down and pay homage to Haman. Everyone complied except for Mordecai. As a Jew, he was to bow to no one except God in obedience to His commandments. The other servants questioned why he would not bow, and he explained that, as a Jew, he was forbidden to bow to anyone. So, they inquired of Haman to see what he had to say.

Haman was furious but was careful in his dealings with Mordecai. This sinistrous individual thought up a plot to have not only Mordecai but all his people throughout the kingdom exterminated. He was not only coming against the Jews but against God as well. In the month of Nisan, the first month of King Ahasuerus's twelfth year of reigning, Haman's followers cast lots (Pur) daily and monthly. They continued doing this until the twelfth month, Adar. They did this for a year, and the king knew nothing of it. This ritual had a two-fold purpose. First, Haman used it to determine the date for his plan to exterminate the Jews. Secondly, it was a spell Haman would use to manipulate the king to agree to his scheme. The king did not know, but God knew.

Haman approached the king with his plan and carefully persuaded him that there was a particular race of individuals whose laws differed from everyone else, and they did not follow the king's laws. They were a rebel group and, as such, needed to be dealt with. Haman suggested they be destroyed and offered to foot the bill, 10,000 talents of silver. It is estimated to have been in the millions of dollars by today's standards. He promised he would put the money into the king's treasury. Just like that, the king took off his signet ring, and after placing it on Haman's finger, he decided that the money and the people would remain at Haman's discretion. He could do with them as he pleased. To achieve such an elevated position within the kingdom in such a fleeting time required an incredible display of charm, wits, and conniving. And then to advance to destroy a particular group of people because one of them would not pay homage to him is evidence enough of an immature, spoiled-rotten child. The evil plot against Mordecai and the Jews in Haman's mind was about to go off without a hitch.

The king's scribes gathered once again to write out a mandate according to all Haman had commanded and address it to all the satraps and governors of all the provinces, in every language of all the people, in the king's name and sealed with the king's signet ring. The letters were then sent by couriers to all the provinces, with instructions to kill all Jews, both young and old, including women and children, on the thirteenth day of Adar, which is the twelfth month. Their enemies would also be permitted to plunder their land. The spell seemed to have worked, as we can see how the king did not hesitate to grant Haman's wish of destruction upon the Jewish people. By the end of the chapter, as news of this event reaches the ears of the people and causes turmoil, the king and Haman sit down and drink.

***

"When Mordecai learned all that had been done, Mordecai tore his clothes and put on sackcloth and ashes, and went out into the midst of the city, and he cried out with a loud and bitter cry" (Esth 4:1).

I can only sympathize with Mordecai as he became aware of the impending threat against him and his people. He tore his clothes and put on sackcloth, crying out and weeping in despair throughout the city. He could only stand outside the king's gate, for no one was permitted to enter while wearing sackcloth. This scene was repeated over and over in all the provinces as many Jews began weeping and mourning their looming fate of extermination, many taking to the streets in sackcloth and ashes, finding no recourse to ease their fears. Esther's handmaidens and

16

eunuchs came to her and conveyed to her what was happening. In her distress, she sent clothes to Mordecai to take off the sackcloth, but he refused. Desiring to find out more about what had happened, Esther sent Hathach, the king's eunuch, to him.

Mordecai explained all that had happened to him, and the amount of money Haman had offered to pay the king to destroy the Jews. He gave him a copy of the written decree to show Esther and explain it to her. He insisted she go before the king to plead on behalf of her people. Hathach returned to Esther with Mordecai's explanation and request. She answered with a reminder that the protocol mandated that no one could enter the inner court unless invited by the king and his golden scepter held out to them upon the pain of death. And the king had not called for Esther to come to him for 30 days. Mordecai responded that she would not be able to escape the fate of her people by hiding in the palace. If she remained silent, somehow, the Jews would still be delivered, but she would surely lose her life.

Mordecai's final question- "*And who knows whether you have not come to the kingdom for such a time as this?*" drove the message home to Esther's heart. Her reply clearly showed that she had come to terms with the thought of undertaking this challenging task. She asked Mordecai to gather all the Jews in Susa to hold a fast on her behalf for three days, neither eating nor drinking, and she would also fast with her handmaidens. Then she would go before the king, knowing she might be risking her life. Maybe the thought that she had support from Mordecai and her people fueled her courage to face this unavoidable battle. However, she also knew in Whom her most excellent support resided. With this action plan in mind, Mordecai set out to obey Esther's orders. "*If my people who are called by my name humble themselves and pray and seek my face and turn from their wicked ways, then I will hear from heaven and will forgive their sin and heal their land*" (2 Chr 7:14). "*When the righteous cry for help, the Lord hears and delivers them out of all their troubles*" (Ps 34:17).

THREE

"On the third day, Esther put on her royal robes and stood in the inner court of the king's palace, in front of the king's quarters, while the king was sitting on his royal throne inside the throne room opposite the entrance to the palace" (Esth 5:1).

On the third day of the fast, Esther put on her royal robes and stood in the king's inner court as the king sat on his throne. With years of preparation and the grace of God upon her, Esther straightforwardly followed His divine instructions. Upon seeing Esther in the courtyard, she again found favor in the king's sight, and he held out his golden scepter. She approached the king and touched the tip of the scepter. The king asked her what her request was. Such was the love he had for her that he was willing to give her half the kingdom. She invited the king and Haman to a feast that she was preparing. The king quickly ordered Haman to be made aware of the invite. Later, as they finished dining and had their wine, the king asked the queen what her wish was. He promised her whatever it was, it would be fulfilled. He offered her half his kingdom. Queen Esther answered that her wish and request was that the king and Haman attend another feast the next day, and then she would reveal her request to the king.

We can speculate what the king was thinking at this point. Something was up, and he would have to wait until the next day. Meanwhile, Haman was delighted to know he was exclusively invited to another feast with His Majesty and the queen. But as he made his way home, he caught sight of Mordecai, who did not rise in honor of him. First, he would not bow; now, he would not rise to his feet. Mordecai had become a nuisance and needed to be dealt with. For now, it was time to head home and enjoy a brag session with his family and friends. And that is what he did. With his great wealth, sons, promotions, and the king promoting him above all the officials, it seemed he had it all. The queen had invited only him and the king to her feast. Yes, life was grand. He was celebrating. It would be perfect if it were not for the one called Mordecai. What would he give never to have to see him again? His wife Zeresh suggested that he have fifty cubit-high gallows built, and in the morning, go before the king and urge him to hang Mordecai on it. Then, go on and enjoy the feast. A look of dark pleasure spread on Haman's countenance. He ordered it to be constructed.

***

"On that night, the king could not sleep. And he gave orders to bring the book of memorable deeds, the chronicles, and they were read before the king" (Esth 6:1).

That same night, the king could not sleep and ordered the chronicles to be brought. After they came to where it described the time Mordecai had saved the king's life by uncovering an assassination attempt by two of his eunuchs, the king asked what honor had been bestowed upon him. "Nothing," responded his servants. The king inquired who was in the courtyard. Haman was in the courtyard, intending to ask the king to hang Mordecai on the gallows. Upon hearing it was Haman, he had him ushered in.

Before Haman could begin his request, the king asked him what should be done for the man the king found delight in. Haman automatically assumed the king was referring to him. With great anticipation, Haman suggested in brilliant detail the following: let the king's royal robes, the horse the king rides upon, and the royal crown be given to the king's most noble official so that he may dress the man to be honored. Then, let that official lead the man on the king's horse through the city square and proclaim, "Thus shall it be done to the man whom the king delights to honor."

King Ahasuerus was pleased and told Haman to do all that he suggested to Mordecai, the Jew who sat at the king's gate, and to be certain to follow through with everything he had recommended. So,

Haman took the royal robe, royal crown, and the king's horse and did as the king ordered. He led Mordecai through the city, proclaiming before the crowd assembled. Upon completing this homage, Mordecai returned to the king's gate while Haman quickly and shamefully headed home. At this point in the story, I found it hard not to laugh. Upon hearing the events, his wife and friends warned him that he had failed in his desire to destroy Mordecai and would now lose his place of honor. While they were speaking, the king's servants arrived to take Haman to the feast Esther had prepared.

FOUR

"So, the king and Haman went in to feast with Queen Esther" (Esth 7:1).

Everything begins to accelerate, and Haman barely has time to consider the situation. He was humiliated by having to parade his arch-rival around on the royal horse in public, no less than on order by the king. His wife and friends further reinforce his internal fear that his time is up. As he headed to the queen's feast, his only comfort was hoping it would end on a brighter note.

As the evening progressed and they drank wine, again the king asked Esther what her wish was, assuring her it would be granted. Even if she requested half the kingdom, he would not deny it.

The moment had arrived for her to finally plead her case before the king for the lives of her people and herself. As the king anxiously gazed upon his beautiful wife, wanting to grant whatever her heart desired, what he heard was not what he expected. Enraged, he asked who it was that dared to want his queen's death. In a flash, the queen signaled to Haman, calling him for what he was: a wicked enemy and an adversary. King Ahasuerus arose and went to the garden as Haman remained before Esther. He was terrified, and now it was his turn to plead for his life. When the king returned, he was infuriated at the sight of Haman groveling before the queen. "Will he molest the queen in my presence?" shouted the king. Harbona, the king's eunuch in attendance, told the king about the gallows that Haman had ordered built to hang Mordecai, who saved the king's life. Haman's fate was sealed. "Hang him on it," ordered the king. With that, Haman was hanged, and the king's anger subsided. The night did not end well for Haman. The trap he had set for Mordecai became his own. *"He makes a pit, digging it out, and falls into the hole that he has made. His mischief returns upon his head, and on his skull his violence descends"* (Ps 7:15-16). *"Whoever digs a pit will fall into it, and a stone will come back on him who starts it rolling"* (Prov 26:27).

***

"On that day, King Ahasuerus gave to Queen Esther the house of Haman, the enemy of the Jews. And Mordecai came before the king, for Esther had told what he was to her" (Esth 8:1).

With Haman gone, a time of tranquility spread throughout the Persian empire. King Ahasuerus entrusted Haman's house to Queen Esther's hands. She then introduced Mordecai as her guardian and explained their relationship. It was not difficult to trust these two, as he had already experienced both Esther and Mordecai's loyalty toward him. He took the signet ring he had given Haman and officially handed it to Mordecai. Esther also set Mordecai to administer over Haman's house. With these formalities in place, the queen then focused her attention on the still-looming day of the extermination of the Jews. She knelt before the king and wept as she begged for the lives of her people. The king held out his royal scepter to her, and she arose.

She requested that he order a revocation of the letter Haman had written regarding the destruction of the Jews. The king responded by first reminding them how he had given custody of Haman's house to Esther and Haman had been hanged on the gallows because he had intended to exterminate the Jews. Haman's house had been entrusted into their custody. He then authorized them to write another edict regarding the Jews in the king's name and the seal of the signet ring, for with the signet ring, it could not be revoked. On the twenty-third day of the month of Sivan, the scribes were summoned. They were instructed to write an edict under Mordecai's guidance to all 127 provinces in each language and the Jews in their language. Couriers took the letters on swift horses used for the king's service. The letters stated that the Jews had permission to defend themselves against any armed force from any province that might attack them on the thirteenth day of Adar, which was the twelfth month. Each province was to receive this decree and publicly display it. The Jews were to be ready to defend themselves on that day. The couriers went out swiftly and conducted their mission. Mordecai went out in royal robes of blue and white, a great golden crown, and another robe of fine linen and purple, and everyone shouted with gladness and joy. As each province received the proclamation and it was read, the Jews were filled with gladness and celebrated with feasting and a holiday. Not only that, but many non-Jews declared themselves Jews, for the fear of the Jews had befallen them.

FIVE

"Now in the twelfth month, which is the month of Adar, on the thirteenth day of the same, when the king's command and edict were about to be carried out, on the very day when the enemies of the Jews hoped to gain the mastery over them, the reverse occurred: the Jews gained mastery over those who hated them" (Esth 9:1).

The Jews prepared themselves for the day Haman had intended to be their extinction. Besides arming themselves with weapons, they prepared spiritually with prayer and fasting. They knew this level of warfare would require their all. On the thirteenth day of Adar, as the Jews gathered in each province and town, ready to defend themselves, their enemies were overcome with fear. The leaders of the provinces had stepped in to protect them because of Mordecai. After Mordecai received the king's promotion to become Prime Minister, he had increased in his authority, spreading his fame throughout the provinces. He became increasingly powerful. A reversal had occurred. I can only attribute it to God. It's as if the enemies recognized God's blessing, approval, and protection of Mordecai. They could not resist and were defeated and destroyed by the Jews.

In Susa, the Jews killed five hundred men, as well as Haman's ten sons. News of that victory reached the ears of the king. He then reported it to Esther. The king displayed joy and asked her what else she wished for. Esther requested the ten sons of Haman be hanged on the gallows the following day. The king issued a decree, and it was carried out. The next day, an additional three hundred men were killed in Susa. A total of 75,000 of those who hated the Jews were defeated and killed, but their lands were not taken. Throughout the provinces, the Jews rested on the fourteenth day and made it a day to celebrate with feasting and gladness. But in Susa, since they were still battling their enemies on the thirteenth and fourteenth, they also rested on the fifteenth with feasting. This is why the Jews in rural areas commemorate the fourteenth day of Adar by feasting and giving food portions to one another.

Then, Mordecai archived this event and decreed that all Jews in all the provinces were to observe the fourteenth and fifteenth day of Adar yearly as the days they were delivered of their enemies. The purpose would be to commemorate how their sorrow and mourning had turned into gladness and celebration, and those days would be spent feasting and giving gifts to people experiencing poverty. Due to their initial response and Mordecai's decree, it became a time of remembrance.

The Feast of Purim, therefore, came about because of Haman the Agagite's plot against the Jews to extinguish them. He used the casting of Pur (cast lots) to destroy them. After discovering the plot, the king ordered Haman and his sons to be exterminated. They were all hanged on the gallows. From this event, we get the word Purim from the term Pur. Thus, the Jews committed to keep this holiday every year as a reminder, even throughout their generations. The Queen and Mordecai then gave their full authority by confirming with a written decree. The decree was sent to all 127 provinces and archived.

***

"King Ahasuerus imposed a tax on the land and the coastlands of the sea" (Esth 10:1).

After these things, King Ahasuerus imposed taxes throughout his kingdom. All his acts and accomplishments, including the promotion of Mordecai, are recorded in the Book of the Chronicles of the Kings of Media and Persia. Mordecai, the Jew, became second in command to the King and was great in the sight of his people. He was popular among them because he sought their welfare and maintained peace.

SIX

CHARACTERS

King Ahasuerus

King Ahasuerus, also known as King Artaxerxes, I and King Xerxes I, was the ruler of the vast Persian empire. *"In a multitude of people is the glory of a king, but without people, a prince is ruined"* (Prov 14:28). As king of such an expansive rulership, he had to protect and maintain his authority. His advisers required wisdom and an important level of understanding concerning relations with neighboring nations. *"A wise man is full of strength, and a man of knowledge enhances his might, for by wise guidance you can wage your war, and in abundance of counselors there is victory"* (Prov 24:5-6). *"Plans are established by counsel; by wise guidance wage war"* (Prov 20:18).

With this in mind, he had to be aware of the continual risk of an internal threat within his ranks. He needed to ensure his circle of royal attendants and advisers were loyal and trustworthy. The king needed to be keen, a reader of character, and brave enough to weed out any menace should it present itself. *"A servant who deals wisely has the king's favor, but his wrath falls on one who acts shamefully"* (Prov 14:35). *"A king who sits on the throne of judgment winnows all evil with his eyes"* (Prov 20:8). *"If a ruler listens to falsehood, all his officials will be wicked"* (Prov 29:12).

King Ahasuerus possessed an impressive gift of generosity. His style of celebrating with those in his realm was elaborate and splendorous. During Esther's feast and coronation, he granted a remission of taxes to the provinces and gave gifts with royal liberality. God significantly blessed him because of his generous spirit. *"The generous man shall be prosperous and enriched, and he who waters will himself be watered"* (Prov 11:25). *"He who is generous will be blessed..."* (Prov 22:9). *"If a king faithfully judges the poor, his throne will be established forever"* (Prov 29:14). There is a downside to being generous, however, which, in the case of King Ahasuerus, could have attracted the takers who manipulated him. As the story progresses, they are revealed and replaced by upright and loyal persons who prove themselves worthy of standing by the king's side to assist him.

He was wisely accommodating to others. In every instance, he treated others respectfully by listening carefully before deciding. *"Let the wise hear and increase in learning, and the one who understands obtain guidance"* (Prov 1:5). *"If one gives an answer before he hears, it is his folly and shame"* (Prov 18:13).

He was a loving and attentive husband. He desired his queen by his side. He offered half his kingdom to Esther. *"Husbands, love your wives, and do not be harsh with them"* (Col 3:19). *"Steadfast love and faithfulness preserve the king, and by steadfast love his throne is upheld"* (Prov 20:28). *"The king's heart is a stream of water in the hand of the Lord; he turns it wherever he will"* (Prov 21:1).

He was passionate about his celebrations and his execution of justice. Anyone attempting to exterminate the king and his queen was met with severe consequences, including those who tried to kill the Jews. *"One who wanders from the way of good sense will rest in the assembly of the dead"* (Prov 21:16). *"The terror of a king is like the growling of a lion; whoever provokes him to anger forfeits his life"* (Prov 20:2). *"A king's wrath is a messenger of death, and a wise man will appease it"* (Prov 16:14). *"Take away the wicked from the presence of the king, and his throne will be established in righteousness"* (Prov 25:5).

King Ahasuerus demonstrated a level of humility that made his rulership uniquely appealing. He had no qualms delegating any administration to those by his side—for example, Haman and later Esther and Mordecai. He didn't demonstrate insecurity but rather maturity. The king's character progressed in his relationships and understanding.

King Ahasuerus's inclination toward strong drinks could potentially incur significant consequences. As I stated, many were looking for the opportunity to overthrow him and take his throne. In a state of drunkenness, his reasoning and capabilities could be clouded and easily manipulated to affect him and his people. For these reasons, limiting wine consumption was essential to maintaining his protection and security as ruler. *"It is not for kings, O Lemuel, it is not for kings to drink wine, or for rulers to take strong drink, lest they drink and forget what has been decreed and pervert the rights of all the afflicted. Open your mouth for the mute, for the rights of all destitute. Open your mouth, judge righteously, defend the rights of the poor and needy"* (Prov 31:4-5, 8-9).

***

Queen Vashti

Queen Vashti's mention was brief because she was more of a placeholder in the story. Her physical beauty was her only investment in her function as queen. This shallowness became apparent when she gathered the women in her exclusive feast. She demonstrated herself to be self-centered, entitled, and manipulative. She should have been by the king's side. Her disinterest and disrespect for the king became evident with that act and, eventually, her refusal to appear at the king's feast. She wanted to enjoy the luxury of being queen without fulfilling her role as wife and queen. She essentially conveyed that her character was below the royal standard. Based on the response from the king's advisers, all present seemed to agree with the king's displeasure. I've heard she may have felt uncomfortable appearing before all those gathered to show off her beauty, so she refused. Nothing could be further from the truth. She was the queen, along with her husband, of a vast empire. She was familiar with the demand for visibility in such a prominent position. By refusing his request, she made it clear to everyone that she did not want to be by the king's side. She wasn't the right fit, and King Ahasuerus finally saw the truth. *"The wisest of women builds her house, but folly with her own hands tears it down"* (Prov14:1).

***

28

Queen Esther

Her real name was Hadassah. Mordecai raised Esther after she was orphaned. Although many Jews had returned to Jerusalem, she remained with Mordecai in Susa. Described as beautiful and well-favored, Esther also possessed humility. She could adapt to the lifestyle of the Persians but not lose touch with her heritage. That characteristic pushed her to the forefront, and with God's help, Esther rose to be the queen of an empire.

She gained the trust and admiration of the king to the extent that he offered her half his kingdom repeatedly. As queen, she continually sought the king's authorization and remained by his side throughout his reign. Her loyalty and love paid off overall. Her attitude proved that obtaining and maintaining a queen's position took more than physical attractiveness. She displayed courage and wisdom when she approached the king on behalf of her people. *"An excellent wife is the crown of her husband, but she who brings shame is like rottenness in his bones"* (Prov 12:4). *"A gracious woman gets honor, and violent men get riches"* (Prov 11:16). *"He who loves purity of heart, and whose speech is gracious, will have the king as his friend"* (Prov 22:11).

Within the Persian culture and many others, there is a tendency for women to be treated as objects, and the king followed that protocol at the beginning of his reign. God began shaking things up. As I previously stated, the shaking allowed the removal of the previous protocol to establish a new protocol. With the advancement of Queen Esther, who demonstrated a superior spirit, connection, understanding, and effort to rise to the occasion, the king's perspective and expectations changed. Being queen took on a whole new meaning. She wasn't just a trophy. She was a trusted advisor and assistant. That was the king's desire, and God brought it to fruition.

***

Haman

Haman the Agagite was a descendant of King Agag, the Amalekite king during the time of King Saul. God had commanded Saul to eliminate the Amalekites. He was not to spare any of them. Saul fought them but spared the king and some animals, later used as sacrifices. When Samuel the prophet came by to see if Saul had fulfilled God's command, he heard the bleating of sheep. He asked him if he had done what he was supposed to, and Saul gave flimsy excuses. In the end, God removed the kingship from him. Because the Amalekites were bent on destroying the Israelites, God wanted them all exterminated. And it ended up that a descendant from Agag survived and continued his lineage. Because of this act of disobedience on Saul's part, Haman later appeared on the scene to finish the job that Agag had failed to do.

The truth is Haman was a narcissist. His selfish, manipulative, self-centered, boastful, and immature ego wanted to be at the top at all costs, even if it meant removing others from this life. *"Everyone who is arrogant in heart is an abomination to the Lord; be assured, he will not go unpunished"* (Prov 16:5). He schemed and used deceptive means to win the king's approval, with his eyes set on the throne. At times, it seemed he was succeeding in this evil intent, and he would've accomplished it if it had not been for God's intervention. *"When wickedness comes, contempt comes also, and with dishonor comes disgrace"* (Prov 18:3). *"Pride goes before destruction, and a haughty spirit before a fall"* (Prov 16:18).

He used astrology, based on his use of Pur, to determine the date for the destruction of the Jews. Combined with his evil, conniving, vindictive, and sinister ways, had he not been exposed, he would've overthrown the king, for that was his goal. *"The house of the wicked will be destroyed, but the tent of the upright will flourish"* (Prov 14:11). *"A servant who deals wisely has the king's favor, but his wrath falls on one who acts shamefully"* (Prov 14:35).

**

Mordecai

Interestingly enough, Mordecai was a descendant of Kish, Saul's father, as was Esther. As stated earlier, Mordecai took Hadassah or Esther as his own and raised her. They were part of the captives that were taken during the reign of King Jeconiah, King of Judah, by King Nebuchadnezzar of Babylon. The Persians overthrew the Babylonians, and during the reign of Cyrus, the Jews were allowed to return to their homeland. For some reason, Mordecai remained with Hadassah in Susa. God arranged it that way.

Mordecai was compassionate, caring, brave, and wise. He was devoted to God, humble, and looked out for the good of others. Many of these qualities were instilled in Esther's life by her cousin. Amid sorrow and heartache, Mordecai developed resilience and overcame many of life's challenges. *"When it goes well with the righteous, the city rejoices, and when the wicked perish there are shouts of gladness"* (Prov 11:10). *"Whoever goes about slandering reveals secrets, but he who is trustworthy in spirit keeps a thing covered"* (Prov 11:13).

SEVEN

As we can see, The Book of Esther never mentions God. Despite this unique feature, His eternal love, divine timing, and purpose are evident. From eternity past, God foresaw this moment that required His divine intervention to preserve the lineage through which His Son, Jesus Christ, would come. At this precise location, there would be an attempt to destroy the Jews. Satan, always seeking to steal, kill, and destroy, organized a covert attack to achieve this goal. Although King Ahasuerus or Xerxes I was the ruler of the great Persian empire, a known pagan culture, God carefully selected him. He had enough good qualities that, combined with two unlikely individuals by his side to assist him, would succeed in toppling the enemy's plans. *"The Lord has made everything for its purpose, even the wicked for the day of trouble"* (Prov 16:4).

These two unlikely individuals were an exiled Jew named Mordecai and his cousin Hadassah, an orphan he raised as his offspring. God used His people's exile to bring these two to the highest positions attainable in that era. But let's analyze who God trusted to accomplish this great mission.

Mordecai did not have much to look forward to, being far from his homeland. He was a servant, an outsider. On top of that, caring for his young cousin was a calling in itself. Hadassah needed comfort, protection, and guidance in a pagan environment. She would need instruction to maintain their Jewish heritage. Did they face discrimination? Would they be able to practice their religion freely? With these and more challenges, they continued daily with faith in the eternal God. They were placed in a place and situation unknown to them at that time that would catapult them to a place of high honor and visibility beyond their wildest dreams. God is so strategic. One of God's well-known methods is using the humble and unknown to accomplish remarkable things for His purposes. *"But God chose what is foolish in the world to shame the wise; God chose what is weak in the world to shame the strong; God chose what is low and despised in the world, even things that are not, to bring to nothing things that are,"* (1 Cor 1:27-28). No one would guess what these two would accomplish and the power they carried within them to change the outcome for them and their fellow exiles. Neither Mordecai nor Esther had a clue as to what the following years held in store for them. While they were busy living their lives in the citadel of Susa, God was busy setting them up for their eventual elevation. *"And we know that for those who love God all things work together for good, for those who are called according to his purpose"* (Rom 8:28).

The timing was essential for this plan to come about. Since God knew that Queen Vashti was a hindrance and could not manage this assignment, what better way to reveal her disinterest in queenly matters than to have her ignore the king's request in the public arena? Everyone would see for themself, and this would allow for her dethroning.

As the search for a new queen proceeded, God had to work on the king's heart. He was heartbroken. His Majesty also needed to adjust his manly perception of what a wife/queen should be like. All this time, he had focused on physical beauty. Perhaps he realized he needed someone with certain inner qualities by his side—someone who possessed wisdom, compassion, understanding, humility, kindness, and loyalty. As the days passed, King Ahasuerus began distinguishing the woman he would set the royal crown upon. Regardless of the number of relationships he had in the past, they were all counterfeits. They were placeholders and time wasters. This time, he would get it right.

Hadassah, or Esther, as she became known, knew what it was like to go without basic needs and feel inadequate, rejected, lonely, and sorrowful. Her only comfort was having Mordecai teach her, encourage her, and provide her with security and protection as much as he could. His influence upon her would be a pivotal factor in securing the position God had in store for her. Although she had suffered much loss throughout her life, she gained strength, courage, wisdom, hope, and purpose. And this future queen was beautiful, which would be a plus for the king. God could now hand over his daughter to her destiny, knowing she would experience the love and blessings of her king.

All the young women underwent a restrictive beauty process during the selection process, and no contact with outsiders was permitted. There could be no distractions, for this training was the highest order. For some, proper etiquette, manners, beauty treatments for hair and skin, and possibly weight management were introduced. For example, they learned how to address and speak to the king and the royal staff. Others received instructions on confidently walking into any room, properly greeting guests, and dining during meals. Attire and appearance had to be well-maintained and clean. Others may have needed to exercise proper language; perhaps their attitude needed adjusting. Their character required dignity, respect, and self-control. As demanding as it sounds, this was an empire, and the queen's visibility was unavoidable. She was an example to all the women, and the respect she received depended on her manner of behavior and attitude.

This process did have its limitations when it came to matters of the heart. It focused on appearance, image, and behavior. All the protocols would be useless in a crisis without the wisdom and courage to face them. Esther had an advantage over the rest regarding matters of the heart. But it would be four years before the king would meet her. I imagine those four years became repetitive as the king discerned each young woman was not the one. Four years of asking, where is my queen? God had chosen Esther and had already put her as his queen in the king's heart. She was, in essence, his rib. *"So the Lord God caused a deep sleep to fall upon the man, and while he slept took one of his ribs and closed up its place with flesh. And the rib that the Lord God had taken from the man he made into a woman and brought her to the man"* (Gen 2:21-22). He would know when the moment arrived for her meeting with him. *"...I am the Lord; in its time I will hasten it"* (Isa 60:22).

When Esther finally went before King Ahasuerus, he knew. He felt butterflies in his stomach; his heart raced, and love flowed through his veins. His royal highness felt things he had never felt before. He fell in love with her instantly and loved her as well. He was so delighted and taken with her that he set the royal crown upon her head. Here stood his queen, the one he had been waiting for. God had signed, sealed, and delivered His wonderful gift to the king, to treasure and love like no other had ever done. Esther's feast was prepared and celebrated among the officials as her welcome. Everyone received gifts from the king. It was a joyous occasion. It was a sign of Divine favor at work. *"Righteous lips are the delight of a king, and he loves him who speaks what is right"* (Prov 16:13).

Shortly after, Esther's first test of loyalty occurred while Mordecai sat at the king's gate. He overheard two eunuchs discussing a plan to assassinate the king. He quickly conveyed the message to Esther, who delivered it to the king. The two would-be assassins were hanged, and details of the plot were recorded in the Chronicles of the King in the presence of His Majesty. The king noticed Esther's commitment to him, confirming that he had made the right choice.

As a side note, it is puzzling that among all the palace staff, not one approached the king to warn him about the threat against him. It took a stranger such as Mordecai to reveal the plot. If Mordecai had not been present, King Ahasuerus most likely would have been assassinated, and who knows how this story would have ended. Here, we see God's grace and mercy towards the king and His people.

EIGHT

All was well with Esther as she settled into life at the palace. The preparation beforehand paid off, and she adjusted to fulfilling her duties as queen. Mordecai came by occasionally to inquire about how she was doing and saw her growth and progress. He may have wondered how marvelous all had turned out for her now in the palace beside the ruler of the Persians. It, indeed, was a dream that he never imagined would come true.

As with all good stories, true life has taught us that there will always be some moments of discouraging events lurking around the corner. Such was the case four years later when the king promoted Haman to second in command, which became a turning point in this story.

Let's pull back the curtain for a moment. Esther was chosen as queen not a moment too soon. When God positions people, He does it rightfully without secret maneuvers or fakery. Esther was authentic; she had no hidden motives and didn't even seek the position. As time passed, there was evidence of her sound and pure heart. Many loved Esther, and there is no evidence that anyone bowed to her, nor did she require it from anyone.

The enemy was also behind the scenes, setting up another counterfeit to advance into a prominent position in the royal court. There was indeed some masterminding and scheming involved in this counterfeit, Haman's, advancement. The first biblical text that follows his promotion states that the king commanded everyone to bow to him—a test for Mordecai, Esther, and the rest of the Jewish population for sure. For the Jews, bowing to anyone or an idol would mean breaking the first and second commandments. In Haman's mind, anyone not bowing to him was worthy of death. The setup was to cause a conflict between the king and God's people, leading to a battle between good and evil. Satan, who is the author of death and destruction, aimed his arrows at bringing down the whole kingdom if possible. It began subtly. Satan had chosen someone who could skillfully and covertly start a campaign of compromise and deception. Haman had a charming public persona. He was well-spoken, cunning, and persistent. He knew that to advance, he needed to take out any threats and anyone who stood in the way. Haman was serious in his intent and would have his way no matter what.

As time passed and the king's servants witnessed Mordecai not bowing to anyone, especially Haman, they reprimanded him daily. It became an obsession. They reminded him it was the law. Even though he told them it went against his religious beliefs as a Jew, they were not satisfied. They decided to take it up to Haman. He was furious when he discovered someone dared not obey the king's command to bow.

Who was this Mordecai? The audacity, the nerve to think he could get away with not paying homage to the king's right-hand man! Upon learning that Mordecai was a Jew, Haman decided not to waste his time eliminating just him. He would take care of all of them. That's right. He would exterminate all of the Jews within the Persian empire. Never mind that none were criminals or people known to create chaos among the populace. They lived a simple lifestyle. They didn't bother anyone. But now they were made out to be the worst of the worst. *"The wicked watches for the righteous and seeks to put him to death"* (Psa 37:32).

Haman cast lots for a year to determine what date could be used for the extermination of the Jews without the king's knowledge. A customary practice among astrologists, he possibly wanted to figure out the day when his "enemies," the Jews, would be at their weakest or most vulnerable. The thirteenth of Adar, which was the twelfth month, became the appointed day to conduct the genocide against the Jews. Looking back in history, one may observe multiple attempts against the people of God, and each one failed. I will add that it did not end well for each perpetrator.

Haman used all his power of persuasion to convince the king to agree with his plan to destroy the Jews, and it worked. He claimed this race of outsiders were troublemakers and didn't follow the laws of the land. His suggestion was to kill them all off and plunder their properties. He was willing to pay into the king's treasury 10,000 talents of silver. Without so much as blinking, the king removed his signet ring and gave it to Haman.

He even told him to keep his money and do what he pleased. Haman could barely conceal his devious pleasure. All his planning, scheming, and even whatever rituals he carried out had worked. He felt like celebrating. The excitement was so overwhelming. He would be rid of Mordecai and these worthless peasants. His plan to reach the top and receive the honor he deserved was at last his, and his alone. Or so he thought.

The king's scribes were called to begin writing the decree for the destruction of the Jews on the thirteenth day of Adar and sent out by couriers to all the provinces, including Susa, the citadel. In every province, cries of disbelief and mourning rang out as the Jewish subjects tried to come to grips with the fate that would befall them. Meanwhile, acting as if all was well, the king and Haman sat down and enjoyed a drink. What just happened?

The king fell into a trap. The enemy had blindsided him. Satan had declared war, and now it was up to Mordecai and Esther to respond with a more significant comeback. God knew all this would happen. That is why he placed Mordecai and Esther in a position to apply a successful counterstrike. Everything was going as planned.

NINE

At first, the queen was unaware that Haman had prepared a death decree against her people. Lately, she had noticed that the king had been constantly occupied with Haman over trivial matters. There was a distance building between them, and it left her troubled in spirit. She brushed it off as just a part of royal duties, but there was a nagging feeling in her that something was not right. Esther hoped things would return to normalcy.

As she returned to her royal quarters, some maidservants approached her with the news that Mordecai was in an unrecognizable state at the king's gate, weeping and dressed in sackcloth and ashes. Knowing about Mordecai's distress greatly disturbed her, and she sent him some garments. Mordecai refused the garments and sent them back to the queen. Puzzled, she called one of the king's eunuchs, Hathach, and sent him to Mordecai to inquire about his distress. Mordecai explained all that Haman had conspired against his and Esther's people. He gave him a copy of the written decree to show and explain to her. It was then that she discovered the Jewish people were marked for extermination. He also insisted that she go before the king to plead on behalf of the Jewish people.

After taking it all in, Esther responded that the king had not requested her presence for 30 days. She could not go before him without his permission. Previously, Esther's presence was a godly influence in King Ahasuerus's life. He functioned better, and his rulership had improved. Everyone else noticed it as well. As Haman stepped into the picture, chaos and dysfunction began seeping in.

Mordecai, who had glimpsed the real Haman, understood that it was up to the queen to speak to the king and plead for their lives. His response has inspired many of us to reflect on our life's purpose. He told her that she could try to hide in the palace and ignore the plight of her people. God would raise another to save them, but she would perish. Then he said the words that captivated her to the point of accepting the call of God on her life. *"And who knows whether you have not come to the kingdom for such a time as this?"* She realized that her life was no accident or coincidence. Considering everything she had endured and now living as a queen made her see it all served a far greater purpose. With firm resolve, she asked him to gather the Jews living in Susa to do a three-day fast, and she said she would do the same with the handmaidens in the palace. Then, she would go to the king. If she perished, she perished. With this determination, Mordecai went his way to do as she asked.

I believe in those three days of fasting, God revealed to Esther the spiritual battle that was taking place. *"Call to me and I will answer you and will tell you great and hidden things that you have not known"* (Jer 33:3). She realized that her role as queen was more than just her daily tasks and duties. She was a major influence on her husband. As king, his overall state of being directly impacted the empire because it was under his rulership. At that moment, she could see that an alien hold or manipulation over the king was leading him toward loss and destruction. *"It is an abomination to kings to do evil, for the throne is established by righteousness"* (Prov 16:12).

Haman, by gaining the king's trust, succeeded in acquiring the promotion that, in his mind, he could use to unseat the king. He desired the royal crown. His narcissism had begun to show itself, and he needed to move quickly. And this is how he would accomplish his goal—first, he kept the king distracted and isolated to create confusion. Then, he began a smear campaign against all those close to the king, including Esther, to cause division and keep the king in a delusional state. Interestingly, King Ahasuerus had no problems with the Jews until now because Haman said so. Because of Haman's continual condemnation of the Jews, the king became convinced that they should be eliminated.

This stronghold had to be rooted out for the kingdom to progress. *"Steadfast love and faithfulness preserve the king, and by steadfast love, his throne is upheld"* (Prov 20:28). As she continued praying and fasting, God gave her the instructions she needed to implement to help the king. God would take care of the rest.

On the third day, three being a significant biblical number, Esther prepared herself to go before the king. As she bathed and dressed in her royal attire, she maintained her thoughts in a peaceful frame. *"You keep him in perfect peace whose mind is stayed on you, because he trusts in you"* (Isa 26:3). She knew what she was up against and was mindful not to let her emotions get the best of her. All the evil seeds of doubt and deception that Haman had planted in the king's mind would be uprooted and replaced with truth, love, and trust once again. As she headed to the inner court of the king's palace, Esther breathed a final prayer to the Almighty, asking for wisdom, strength, and courage to face the challenge she had before her. She kept replacing thoughts of doubt with faith in God, like what David endured when heading out to face Goliath. The intensity of the arrows coming against her must mean the enemy knew he was about to be defeated. It was a fierce battle, but she finally felt a holy power course through her being. She felt the release of the attacks, and she was ready.

She heard her name within minutes of entering the inner court near King Ahasuerus's quarters. She felt a warm tingle as she turned and saw the king holding his golden scepter to her. This was the moment. God's favor covered her as she approached the king and touched the tip of his scepter. She saw the same love in his eyes that she'd seen when he saw her for the first time. It was God; He was doing it again. She instantly understood that everything was turning around and would be all right. *"In the light of a king's face there is life, and his favor is like the clouds that bring the spring rain"* (Prov 16:15).

After inquiring about her, the king asked her what her request was. He offered half the kingdom if that was her wish. It seemed King Ahasuerus had come across many who only sought material goods. It is sad to find oneself surrounded by people who are only your friends or allies based on what you can offer them regarding wealth and favors. His relationships had come to that point. But it was different with Esther. She was so down-to-earth. She was more concerned with people, relationships, and helping others. Maybe not having parents made her understand that those around her had more value than possessions. This quality intrigued him about the queen, and he loved her even more.

She requested that the king and Haman attend a feast that same day. King Ahasuerus sent word to Haman so they would go to the feast the queen was preparing. After enjoying a wonderful meal and drinking the wine afterward, the king turned to Esther and asked her the same question. What was her wish? What was her request? It would be granted, even to half the kingdom. She smiled sweetly and said, *"My wish and request are: if I have found favor in the sight of the king and if it pleases the king to grant my wish and fulfill my request, let the king and Haman come to the feast that I will prepare for them, and tomorrow I will do as the king has said."* The king and Haman looked at one another, shrugged, smiled, and agreed. With such a peaceful atmosphere, Haman dared not ruin it. His deceptive ways had worked, and he had to keep it up until he attained his goal. After bidding one another farewell, the king retired to his quarters. Haman set out with a giddiness he could barely contain; due to the wine and the excitement, he felt everything was going as planned. It wasn't until he reached the king's gate that his happiness turned to rage.

TEN

The sight of Mordecai sitting there, neither rising nor trembling in his presence, rattled him to the core. *"The wicked man sees it and is angry; he gnashes his teeth and melts away; the desire of the wicked will perish"* (Psa 112 :10)! Nevertheless, he let it slide and continued on his way home. There, he gathered his friends, and with his wife, Zeresh, he recounted his great wealth, the number of sons he had, his promotions by the king, and how he had advanced above all the other officials and servants at the palace. He shared with them about the feast the queen had prepared for only him and the king and how she again invited them both to another one the next day. But he was still not satisfied with all that he acquired. Nothing would bring greater pleasure than not having to see Mordecai sitting at the king's gate.

Mordecai was minding his business, and Haman would have none of it. He could not rest till he made all these nonbeings disappear. I would dare ask, if they were nonbeings, why would you take the time and the effort to eliminate them? Haman and all the narcissists that ever existed and those who still do all carry the same traits. One of the traits is their distorted ego. They wish they had a giant pencil so they could erase certain people. Anyone they perceive as better needs to be removed. In their immaturity, they cannot understand why others do not see it as they do. It is a sad reality that we are living even today. Anyway, Haman couldn't stand Mordecai because he was seeing someone with greatness inside him. And Haman felt threatened by that perception. He wanted to squash him, but he couldn't. Therefore, he concocted a plan to persuade the king to wipe them out. Narcissists like others to do their dirty work and blame them afterward.

After a pause, Haman's wife conceived a "brilliant" idea. She suggested that Haman construct a 75-foot gallows and ask the king to hang Mordecai. Haman's eyes lit up, and he was pleased. He quickly began construction on it.

Later that night, for some reason, King Ahasuerus could not sleep. He bathed, walked out on the terrace to watch the night sky, and then tried again to get some rest. The hours kept ticking by, and he tossed and turned. It finally occurred to him to have one of his eunuchs bring the Chronicles of the Kings and read it to him. That would do the job, he hoped. He began to feel a bit relaxed and drowsy. Suddenly, he sat up. It was during the reading of the part when Mordecai had exposed the assassination attempt by Bigthan and Teresh. He asked what honor Mordecai had received for that act. Nothing was the response. No wonder he could not sleep. King Ahasuerus was known for always recognizing great acts with rewards, but this one had slipped his mind for some reason. How could he forget to honor something like this? He felt the urge to do something extra special for Mordecai, to make up for lost time. He needed to speak to an advisor. "Who is in the courtyard?" he asked. "Haman," responded the young men.

We already know that Haman had gallows constructed to hang Mordecai on them. He had come to the palace to seek the king's permission to conduct his plan. While he waited in the courtyard, the king had just discovered that Mordecai had not been honored for saving the king's life. How's that for Divine timing? Each had a different desire for Mordecai. One wanted to honor him, and the other wanted him dead. Neither knew what the other was desiring. The king told his servants to bring Haman to him. Before Haman could make his request known, the king welcomed him with the following question. What should be done to the man whom the king delights to honor? Haman thought he had won the lottery. Who else could the king want to celebrate in the Persian empire besides Haman? He was the kingdom's most intelligent, qualified, honorable, and worthy. He was second in command to the king. The queen had invited him and the king to two feasts, and now this. It didn't take him long to respond.

He knew what he wanted and suggested the following. *"For the man whom the king delights to honor, let royal robes be brought, which the king has worn, the horse that the king has ridden, and on whose head a royal crown is set. And let the robes and the horse be handed over to one of the king's most noble officials. Let them dress the man whom the king delights to honor and let them lead him on the horse through the square of the city, proclaiming before him: 'Thus shall it be done to the man whom the king delights to honor.'"*

King A had attained much wisdom and humility at this point. He had learned much from Queen Esther. I'm not sure if, at this moment, he could see through to Haman's pride. By allowing him to decide the honor that would be given Mordecai, Haman's desire and true intentions for that honor were exposed. His suggestion for the man to wear all the king's attire, his royal robe and crown, and even ride the royal horse made it clear that Haman not only wanted to wear the king's royal robe and crown and ride his horse but ultimately sit on the royal throne. We can see how the king was not concerned with briefly letting someone wear his attire. He was not greedy, insecure, or self-centered. He didn't have to compete with anyone. He knew his authority and position.

What Haman heard next was like having a bucket of ice-cold water poured over his head. The king ordered him to take all the items he mentioned and do it exactly as he proposed to Mordecai. Did he hear right? Mordecai? He felt like he was about to pass out. He smiled weakly and headed off to fulfill what was to be a most unpleasant task. After Mordecai was dressed and mounted the horse, Haman walked before him, proclaiming loudly, *"Thus shall it be done to the man whom the king delights to honor."* As the people gathered and cheered for Mordecai, Haman did all he could to maintain his composure. He mentally counted the minutes before it would be over. When it had finally ended, Mordecai returned to his post at the king's gate, and Haman headed home in a mortified state. He told his wife, Zeresh, and all his friends what had happened. They came to the same conclusion. Haman's goose was cooked. If Mordecai had been honored by the king, Haman would not be able to get rid of him. It was becoming clear that Haman's plans for Mordecai and the Jews were about to fall upon him. While discussing all this, the king's eunuchs arrived in order to escort Haman to the queen's feast.

I want to point out something important about this story that I've never heard mentioned before. It has to do with God's mercy. God had mercy on Haman by allowing him to repent and turn from his wickedness to Him. Every day, he ignored God's goodness to him and his family.

Although Haman used deceptive means to obtain many promotions and even his great wealth, God allowed it in His permissive will. He experienced more benefits than his peers, yet he was never satisfied. Haman failed to appreciate all the abundance he and his family enjoyed. He wanted more. Being at the top, having more than others, and the recognition and image were the idols he had erected in his heart. That is a dangerous place because he was so full of himself and his earthly ambitions that he had no room for God and His eternal plan of redemption.

ELEVEN

It was time for the queen's feast. She outdid herself on the second day. The food was delicious, and the wine was supreme and elegant. Haman pushed aside the anxious thoughts that invaded his mind after the ordeal with Mordecai. He relished in this moment to nurture his wounded ego. He was at the place where he deserved to be. Then, the king asked Queen Esther what she wished and desired most, even if it were half of the kingdom. This slight pause was a precursor to something suspenseful. Whatever it was, it was building up to the point that it became nerve-wracking for Haman. Both the king and Haman stared at Esther, waiting for her response. *"Then Queen Esther answered, "If I have found favor in your sight, O king, and if it please the king, let my life be granted me for my wish, and my people for my request. For we have been sold, I and my people, to be destroyed, to be killed, and to be annihilated. If we had been sold merely as enslaved people, men, and women, I would have been silent, for our affliction is not to be compared with the loss to the king"* (Esth 7:3-4).

This declaration took the king utterly by surprise. Was someone threatening his queen? Who? She finally exposed him with, "A foe and enemy! This wicked Haman!" Haman felt all the blood drain from his face as Esther pointed directly at him. He could barely breathe; the terror was too great. *"Ah, you destroyer, who yourself have not been destroyed, you traitor, whom none has betrayed! When you have ceased to destroy, you will be destroyed; and when you have finished betraying, they will betray you"* (Isa 33 :1). The king got up in a rage and headed out to the palace garden, leaving the queen and Haman. King A felt the betrayal at once. This evil fellow whom he had taken in as an advisor and confidante. All this time, he had trusted his words. He trusted his image of loyalty and reliability. He believed this con artist to be honest and kind-hearted. The veil had been lifted, and now the king saw Haman for who he indeed was.

While the king headed to the garden, Haman quickly moved towards Esther to beg for his life. He tried all sorts of excuses to no avail. She looked away because she knew his true intentions. He had schemed and plotted against her and her people. She had done nothing to deserve such cruelty, and neither did her people. His insatiable desire to be bowed down to, to be paid homage to, could never nor would ever be satisfied. This was an obsession that the king was about to deal a lethal blow to.

It was too late for Haman. Upon returning to where they had been dining, the king caught sight of Haman nearly on top of Esther, begging her for another chance. In his anger and displeasure, the king could only see Haman as a threat to their peace and cried out, "Will he even assault the queen in my presence, in my own house?" As the cherry on top, Harbona, one of the king's eunuchs, informed the king that the fifty cubit-high gallows that Haman had built to hang Mordecai was standing at Haman's house. Yes, you heard that right, O king. According to Haman, the Mordecai who saved your life was supposed to die by hanging. The king's response? "Hang Haman on it." So, they hanged Haman, and the king's wrath was abated.

It was a remarkable feeling as Esther was released from the burden that weighed upon her shoulders. She no longer had to keep her lineage a secret from the king for fear of rejection. Finally, she felt safe and accepted after the turmoil brought on by Haman. With Haman removed and out of the picture came a new beginning and many changes for the kingdom. The first thing King A did was hand over Haman's house to Queen Esther. The tables began to turn quickly. The queen then called for Mordecai to come to the palace, and she formally introduced him as her cousin, who had raised her as his daughter. This may have been a lot to process for the king, but it also brought more clarity and understanding towards Esther. He may have felt more blessed as he considered the challenges she had faced and the incredible woman she was. His love for his queen grew exponentially.

After meeting the man who had saved his life and seeing his extraordinary influence upon Esther, King A was more than convinced of what he had to do. The king removed the signet ring he had previously retrieved from Haman and gave it to Mordecai. The queen immediately transferred the administration of Haman's house to Mordecai. It became apparent that it was reaping season for Mordecai as he began to reap the blessings of his faithfulness to God. In a matter of hours, Mordecai went from one who sat at the king's gate to the Prime Minister of the Persian Empire. I might add that the subsequent role reversal was very well deserved.

Despite the positive strides they were making in setting up a better administration, there remained the threat that the Jews had yet to face. Queen Esther fell at the king's feet, and weeping, she began to plead again on behalf of her people. She asked that the wicked plan that Haman had devised be averted. King A held out his scepter, and she arose. After composing herself, she asked that an order be written to revoke the decree that Haman had devised to destroy the Jews in all the provinces. She wondered how she could bear to see the calamity that would happen to them. With much concern and compassion toward his wife, the king reiterated the handing over of Haman's house to the queen's hands and the hanging of Haman on the gallows because of his plot against the Jews. He then permitted them to do as they pleased concerning the situation of the Jews, in his name, and to seal it with the king's ring. That way, it would not be revoked since it was written in the king's name and sealed with his ring. With renewed hope and gratitude, Esther's countenance again radiated the joy she felt towards the king's decision. Her people would be safe and be able to face a brighter future now.

On the twenty-third day of the month of Sivan, which is the third month, the king's scribes were gathered. Under dictation by Mordecai, an edict was written to all the satraps and governors of the 127 provinces in the king's name and sealed with the king's signet ring. In it, it stated the king's permission was granted to the Jews to gather and defend themselves on the thirteenth day of Adar, to destroy, kill, and annihilate any attackers, and to plunder their goods. These letters were sent out by couriers mounted on the swift horses used in the king's service. A copy would be issued as a decree to each province and publicly displayed. It was also decreed in the citadel of Susa.

Everything had turned around in a matter of days. The sight of Mordecai dressed in blue and white royal robes, a great golden crown, and a robe of fine linen and purple caused the crowds to shout and rejoice. There was such a celebratory excitement among the Jews as word reached them about the king's ruling. This impacted the rest of the populace to the extent that many of them declared themselves to be Jews out of fear.

What happened during the nine months that remained from the time the decree went out that the Jews could defend themselves to the actual date previously determined to be their extermination? Much preparation was taking place. In response to any attacks by their enemies, the Jews armed themselves with weaponry and trained themselves for the fight of their lives. Although Haman was no longer around, the threat against them remained. He had planted seeds of discord and hate among the citizenries. If left unchecked, the ramifications would cause irreparable damage to the empire. This period of nine months of preparation was also intended for the citizens to reflect on the hate and ill will that they felt towards the Jews. Would they allow Haman's hostility to control their thoughts and actions? Could they see the Jews posed no threat to their well-being? The Jews also prepared spiritually with prayers and fasting. They knew they needed God's strength and power to overcome this future attempt to wipe them out.

TWELVE

The thirteenth day of Adar arrived, and the enemies of the Jews expected to eliminate them, but those who prepared to take them down were taken by surprise. A significant reversal had occurred. The Jews gathered with their weaponry, and their enemies were overtaken by fear. Even the officials, satraps, governors, and royal agents in each province joined the Jews in defending them because of Mordecai. He had increased dramatically in power and authority, and his fame had swept throughout the realm. Amid the fighting, the Jews killed and destroyed all who came against them. In Susa, the citadel, five hundred men were killed. Also killed were the ten sons of Haman, but their properties were not plundered. These numbers were reported to the king, who then relayed them to Queen Esther. He then asked her what she wished, assuring her it would be fulfilled. She asked that the Jews in Susa be given an extra day to complete the job. She also requested that Haman's ten sons be hanged on the gallows. The decree was followed through with the king's permission, and Haman's ten sons were hanged. Someone may question the reason the queen wanted Haman's sons hanged. She desired to show everyone that any further threats would not be tolerated but managed with severity. They represented the instigator of this genocide, their father, and with their removal from life, the Amalekite threat against Israel was finally defeated. On the fourteenth day of Adar, the Jews gathered once again and killed an additional three hundred men in Susa.

It is worth noting that Haman's evil intentions saw enormous consequences. He suffered the loss of his life and his ten sons as well, who were supposed to be his heirs. His wife, Zeresh, lost her husband and sons and their possessions in one moment. She faced shame and embarrassment and became destitute. *"Those who hate you will be clothed with shame, and the tent of the wicked will be no more"* (Job 8:22). Because of his actions, an all-out war and loss of life came as a result. He came to be known as what he had desired upon the Jews and Mordecai: weak, insignificant, miserable, worthless. He ended up where he had wished for them: six feet under. The seat Haman so spitefully fought to gain and maintain was given to Mordecai, the man he envied and desperately tried to destroy. Outside the capital of Susa, in the other provinces, the Jews defended themselves and killed 75,000 men who came against them. The following day, the fourteenth of Adar, they rested and made it a day of feasting and gladness.

In summary, the battle in Susa continued on the thirteenth and fourteenth of Adar. On the fifteenth, they rested and celebrated with feasting and gladness. In the rest of the provinces, the battle was fought solely on the thirteenth of Adar, and they held their feasting and joy on the fourteenth. It was much like a holiday as they sent food and gifts to one another.

Mordecai recorded and archived this event. Letters were then sent to the Jews of each province, stating the fourteenth and fifteenth days of Adar would be dedicated to days of feasting and the giving of food gifts and gifts to people experiencing poverty. This observance was acceptable to the Jews, as they had already begun commemorating these days of celebration. These days became known as Purim, taken from the term Pur. Due to the severity of what they had faced, they committed themselves and their future generations to observe these two days. Seeing the acceptance and agreement of the Jews to memorialize the days of Purim, Queen Esther, and Mordecai gave full written authority with a second letter regarding Purim. This letter was copied and sent to all 127 provinces of the kingdom of Ahasuerus as a reiteration and reminder to all the Jews of the tradition they had committed themselves to.

The finality of the story states that King Ahasuerus imposed a tax on the whole land and the coastlands of the sea. God greatly blessed the Medo-Persian empire during this time in history. There was a need to impose a tax on all to maintain its economy and provide for its residents. The rest of his mighty acts and his promotion of Mordecai to a high honor can be found in the Book of the Chronicles of the Kings of Media and Persia. Mordecai was second in command to the king and became prominent and renowned among his people because he pursued the well-being of his people and maintained peace among them. *"And though your beginning was small, your latter days will be very great"* (Job 8:7). *"His master said to him, 'Well done, good and faithful servant. You have been faithful over a little; I will set you over much. Enter into the joy of your master'"* (Matt 25 :23).

THIRTEEN

LESSONS LEARNED

During the moments I spent in prayer and meditation upon the biblical texts, what stood out to me was the heart of God for people and His role in their daily lives and experiences. I observed the following in the Book of Esther.

1. God's sovereignty is undeniable.

Even when God chose to exclude His name from this text, one can't help but notice He is the direct facilitator throughout. *"Truly, you are a God who hides himself, O God of Israel, the Savior"* (Isa 45:15). This is very much so in our present age; God may appear afar off, in the distance, but in actuality, He is very present in the daily activities of all the inhabitants of this world. *"The eyes of the Lord are in every place, keeping watch on the evil and the good"* (Prov 15:3).

No one can ever claim to understand everything God does. *"For as the heavens are higher than the earth, so are my ways higher than your ways and my thoughts than your thoughts"* (Isa 55:9). *"To whom then will you liken God, or what likeness compare with him?"* (Isa 40:18). The fact that He allowed Haman to rise as Prime minister might not make sense to some people. And then allow him to make a law to exterminate the Jews. Why? We will never understand everything that happens in life. But we can trust in the One who has authority over the matters of all men because He is more than capable of it. In the end, the results speak for themselves. *"Oh, the depth of the riches and wisdom and knowledge of God! How unsearchable are his judgments and how inscrutable his ways! For who has known the mind of the Lord, or who has been his counselor? For from him and through him and to him are all things. To him be glory forever. Amen"* (Rom 11:33-34, 36).

He chose King Ahasuerus to rule the grand Medo-Persian empire because the king had a teachable heart. *"My son, if you receive my words and treasure up my commandments with you, making your ear attentive to wisdom and inclining your heart to understanding; then you will understand the fear of the Lord and find the knowledge of God. For the Lord gives wisdom; from his mouth come knowledge and understanding; he stores up sound wisdom for the upright; he is a shield to those who walk in integrity, guarding the paths of justice and watching over the way of his saints. Then you will understand righteousness and justice and equity, every good path; for wisdom will come into your heart, and knowledge will be pleasant to your soul; discretion will watch over you, understanding will guard you, delivering you from the way of evil, from men of perverted speech, who forsake the paths of uprightness to walk in the ways of darkness, who rejoice in doing evil and delight in the perverseness of evil, men whose paths are crooked, and who are devious in their ways"* (Prov 2:1-2, 5-15) *"I the Lord search the heart and test the mind, to give every man according to his ways, according to the fruit of his deeds."* (Jer 17:10).

He knew King Ahasuerus, with suitable helpers, would lead the kingdom to achieve a time of peace and prosperity where His people could thrive and continue the lineage towards the Messiah. *"He does not withdraw his eyes from the righteous, but with kings on the throne he sets them forever, and they are exalted"* (Job 36:7). Because only God sees the heart and intentions of everyone, He can choose whom He will, to bring about His purposes. We see this repeatedly throughout history. *"Or is God the God of Jews only? Is he not the God of Gentiles also? Yes, of Gentiles also, since God is one—who will justify the circumcised by faith and the uncircumcised through faith"* (Rom 3:29-30).

2. In God's eyes, humility goes before greatness, and pride leads to a downfall.

Four of the five key figures in the Book of Esther end up in a role reversal. King Ahasuerus chose Queen Vashti and Haman for their respective positions of honor, but both failed miserably in faithfulness to him. Each presented a fake image, and, unfortunately, he allowed what his eyes saw to be the deciding factor in his choices. But God allowed it as a learning experience. When God presented His choices, the king saw for himself the difference between them and was able to take satisfaction in the high quality of character of Queen Esther and Mordecai. The empire grew, flourished, and increased in respect among its inhabitants and other nations because of God's favor upon them.

Once again, we can see that, as in many cases throughout the Bible text, the individuals chosen for a specific mission or position came from humble beginnings or were considered unqualified. Examples include Moses, Gideon, and David. This was also the case for both Mordecai and Esther. By outward appearances, Mordecai did not exhibit any unique qualities by society's standards that could earn him a position in the king's court. The reality is, he was exactly who the king needed by his side. It took several years for this to become apparent to the king. Anyone who allows God to choose can always expect the best.

Lacking a degree or having no connections is not a problem in God's eyes. In the world, not everyone has the privilege or the means to obtain a secular preparation. Many people come from lower-income family units. God knows all this. When He steps in, He often overlooks the qualified and chooses someone with no connections to show His grace and favor upon their life. By the time God is done elevating them, many will be amazed at who they become and what they achieve with His help. Mordecai was targeted and put under the microscope by Haman because he considered him small, but God chose to put him on display as someone great because he had learned to oversee such greatness. His humility was the foundation that withstood the weight of greatness.

Besides the four principal characters who underwent role reversals, another reversal is mentioned in chapter nine. The planned extermination of the Jews gave their enemies the upper hand. But the decree that permitted the Jews to defend themselves caused the tables to turn. The Jews became the feared, and their enemies became their underlings.

3. *God rolls up his sleeves when any enemy threatens His own with destruction and defends them.*

In every instance in Bible times, God allowed danger to come against his people up to a certain point, only to show His power to protect them. He used men and sometimes women through different circumstances to show their enemies they could not go beyond His set boundaries. *"God is our refuge and strength, a very present help in trouble"* (Psa 46:1). *"Every word of God proves true; he is a shield to those who take refuge in him"* (Prov 30:5). *"The Lord is good, a stronghold in the day of trouble; he knows those who take refuge in him"* (Nah 1:7)

4. *God uses time to assess character to promote or elevate.*

Patience is a virtue, and it was evident in Mordecai's life. Sitting and sometimes standing at the king's gate was not a comfortable place or position to occupy. Much less when Haman arrived on the scene, who took to persecuting him and his race. But God seemed to have placed him there, requiring him to be still and continue to wait on Him. What else could he do? He could be back in his land with those who had returned, but here he remained, a foreigner at the king's mercy. In time, Mordecai saw the results of his time of waiting and trusting in God. *"Blessed is the one who listens to me, watching daily at my gates, waiting beside my doors"* (Prov 8:34). *"The reward for humility and fear of the Lord is riches, honor, and life"* (Prov 22:4).

Esther also waited patiently before meeting the king. Although the process was for 12 months of beauty treatments, she waited an additional three years, totaling four years. Who knows what she thought whenever a young woman went before the king? Would he choose that one or this one? What were the discussions among them all? Did she ever have moments of doubt? All the time spent waiting was time well spent. It helped in her personal development- spiritual, mental, and emotional. All the unknowns were surrendered to the God who knew what He was doing.

5. Evil will not go unpunished. God, in His divine moment, does bring about righteous judgment.

Haman's appearance and role as the prime villain may serve as a reminder of the presence of evil in someone's life. There is no description of wrongdoing on anyone's part to cause such an absurd reaction from him towards the Jewish people and Mordecai. On the contrary, those around him displayed much patience and tolerance. Queen Esther, throughout her two-day feast, showed kindness towards Haman. How many more opportunities did he need to recognize his wrongful ways and make an about-face towards a better way? He deliberately ignored the chances he was given. Under his leadership as Prime Minister, there was discord, hatred, and a lack of peace. No further growth and advancement could prevail until King Ahasuerus dealt with this disruptor in the kingdom. *"For everyone who exalts himself will be humbled, and he who humbles himself will be exalted"* (Luke 14:11). *"Our God is a God of salvation, and to God, the Lord, belong deliverances from death. But God will strike the heads of his enemies, the hairy crown of him who walks in his guilty ways"* (Psa 68:20-21).

As in times past, there are a substantial amount of "Hamans" in society today. They can be male or female, young or old. They prefer high positions in whatever field they specialize in. After you encounter a narcissist, your life will never be the same. They are deluded individuals who think they are getting away with the misery they inflict on others. Although they may seem to succeed in their destructive behavior, they will come face to face with the consequences. Many call it karma. I'll simply say what you sow is what you reap. *"Whoever sows injustice will reap calamity, and the rod of his fury will fail"* (Prov 22:8). *"As I have seen, those who plow iniquity and sow trouble reap the same"* (Job 4:8). *"Do not be deceived: God is not mocked, for whatever one sows, that will he also reap"* (Gal 6:7).

6. *Good actions and deeds will be rewarded in time as well.*

I believe the adverse circumstances that show themselves contrast the good and the bad. In the example of Vashti, the king felt the lack of a queen by his side. With Esther, her presence, loyalty, wisdom, love, and patience shone brightly, igniting in him a spark of passion and desire that grew ever so much. The same was true for Haman and Mordecai. Mordecai's unassuming leadership role overshadowed Haman's immature approach in his dealings with the populace. King Ahasuerus may have wondered at them, possibly never having experienced such qualities beforehand. Now, we can see it was God's hand upon them. *"Awesome is God from his sanctuary; the God of Israel—he is the one who gives power and strength to his people. Blessed be God"* (Psa 68:35)!

Haman was focused on attaining the highest position in the kingdom and wouldn't allow anyone or anything to stand in his way. He was willing to commit murder and almost did, were it not for God's intervention. Hate, jealousy, envy, and insecurities fueled his obsession, leading to his downfall and eventual destruction. On the other hand, we see Mordecai quietly observing and focusing on God. He may have been living in survival mode, not knowing how all this would turn out. After all, Mordecai was just a foreigner. Again, God had bigger plans for him beyond anything he could have imagined. *"For I know the plans I have for you, declares the Lord, plans for welfare and not for evil, to give you a future and a hope"* (Jer 29:11).

To sum it up, a significant theme in this story is the emphasis on table turning and role reversals. The humbling of the "great" and the elevation of the "small." It is also known as the last shall be first, and the first shall be last. *"And behold, some are last who will be first, and some are first who will be last"* (Luke 13:30). There is a cost for greatness in God's kingdom. When God elevates one of His own, there will tend to be individuals who become hateful, jealous, and envious partly because they didn't see the time God was preparing them for that position. Did anyone care about Mordecai as he sat or stood at the gate? No, not at all. Instead, they criticized him for not bowing down to Haman. He faced moments of persecution, hatred, and mistreatment. God allowed those situations to keep him humble and eventually elevate him. We see Haman did not go through that process and could not maintain the position because he was too proud.

As we can see, the Book of Esther is more than a beauty pageant and more than a love story. In this moment in history, we witness the evident attentiveness and protection of the Sovereign God for His people. As each sequence of events played out, He maintained His plan of redemption by dismantling the enemy's evil schemes. The promise, which began in the Garden of Eden and culminated at the cross of Calvary, would have been made invalid if Haman's wicked purpose to exterminate the Jews had succeeded. We need not fear that God has forgotten us when adverse events and circumstances rage around us because God has promised to fulfill His plans and purposes. *"Then the Lord said to me, "You have seen well, for I am watching over my word to perform it"* (Jer 1:12). In this present time, we will again see specific individuals selected by God to occupy positions of power and authority, in a role reversal. *"...Who will say to Him, 'What are you doing?'"* (Job 9:12). *"He has brought down the mighty from their thrones and exalted those of humble estate;"* (Luke 1:52). *"He raises up the poor from the dust; he lifts the needy from the ash heap to make them sit with princes and inherit a seat of honor. For the pillars of the earth are the Lord's, and on them he has set the world"* (1 Sam 2:8).

FOURTEEN

Esther's story is one of redemption that continues to this present time. This book would not be complete if I didn't share the following: God's preservation of the messianic lineage made way for His Son, Jesus Christ, to come to planet Earth. His thirty-three years here were spent teaching, preaching, healing the sick and afflicted, and freeing many captives. He gave up His life by dying on the cross to provide a means for each one of us to attain eternal life. It was the only way because we are all marred by sin. God's gift of salvation is open to all. Anyone may call upon Him. *"For all have sinned and fall short of the glory of God, and are justified by his grace as a gift, through the redemption that is in Christ Jesus, whom God put forward as a propitiation by his blood, to be received by faith. This was to show God's righteousness, because, in his divine forbearance, he had passed over former sins"* (Rom3:23-25). *"For the wages of sin is death, but the free gift of God is eternal life in Christ Jesus our Lord"* (Rom 6:23). It was an expression of His divine love for all of us. *"For God so loved the world, that he gave his only begotten Son, that whosoever believeth in him should not perish, but have everlasting life"* (John 3:16 KJV).

To you my friend, if you have never received this wonderful gift or perhaps have wandered off from God, I invite you to take a moment to pray this prayer. He is waiting for you with open arms, no matter where you are or what you may have done. He loves you with an eternal love. *"The LORD hath appeared of old unto me, saying, Yea, I have loved thee with an everlasting love: therefore with lovingkindness have I drawn thee"* (Jer 31:3 KJV). Say this prayer- Dear God in Heaven, I recognize I am a sinner. I come to you asking for forgiveness of my sins. I believe in my heart and speak with my mouth that Jesus Christ is your son, who died on the cross for my sins. I confess Jesus as the Lord of my life. I accept Jesus as my savior and praise you for making a way for me. I declare by the blood of Jesus that I am saved. I invite you into my life, Lord, and I pray you fill me with your Holy Spirit. Thank you for the new creation you have made me, in Jesus' Name. Amen.

If you prayed that prayer with your heart, you can be sure God has heard you. You are now His son/daughter and have entered a new life in Him. I welcome you into the family of God and pray you will continue to seek and follow Jesus Christ. *"And it shall come to pass that everyone who calls upon the name of the Lord shall be saved"* (Acts 2:21). *"Therefore, if anyone is in Christ, he is a new creation. The old has passed away; behold, the new has come. All this is from God, who through Christ reconciled us to himself and gave us the ministry of reconciliation; that is, in Christ God was reconciling the world to himself, not counting their trespasses against them, and entrusting to us the message of reconciliation"* (2 Cor 5:17-19). Persistence and consistency are essential in your walk with God. Never give up. *"But the one who endures to the end will be saved"* (Matthew 24:13). I pray you are blessed and enriched by God's Word as you grow closer to our Lord and Savior Jesus Christ.

www.ingramcontent.com/pod-product-compliance
Lightning Source LLC
LaVergne TN
LVHW051429080426
835508LV00022B/3321